Samuel Johnson
Man of Words

ALICIA BRENT

ISBN: 1502570173
ISBN-13: 978-1502570178

AUTHOR'S NOTE

While every effort has been made to ensure the information in this book is correct, human error is always a possibility and the author apologises for any inaccuracies.

CONTENTS

INTRODUCTION

Samuel Johnson, 1709 – 1784, was one of England's major literary figures of the eighteenth century. Born in Lichfield (where the house of his birth still stands), the son of a bookseller and his wife, he suffered ill health early in life and was left with a condition that a hundred years later would be named Tourette's Syndrome, characterised by uncontrollable gestures and tics.

His family were not well off but Samuel was a very bright child and was taught by his mother to read at very early age. It is no surprise, therefore, that he pursued a literary career, publishing numerous poems, essays, biographies and stories and numbering among his acquaintances many of the famous names of the time, including the artist Joshua Reynolds.

His greatest claim to fame today is as the compiler of the first really comprehensive and structured dictionary of the English language, which took him nine years to complete and which was so highly regarded that it was not until the publication in 1928 of the Oxford English Dictionary that it had a serious rival.

Given his literary ability and the quantity of writings he left us, there are many quotations that have been passed down to us to be enjoyed. One of his most frequently recalled is 'Patriotism is the last refuge of a scoundrel.' In this book you will find that one, alongside a selection of others from this master of words.

ABOUT HIMSELF

"Every man who attacks my belief, diminishes in some degree my confidence in it, and therefore makes me uneasy; and I am angry with him who makes me uneasy."

*

"I have found men to be more kind than I expected, and less just."

*

"I never desire to converse with a man who has written more than he has read."

*

"I will be conquered; I will not capitulate."

*

"That we must all die, we always knew; I wish I had remembered it sooner."

*

"I would not give half a guinea to live under one form of government other than another. It is of no moment to the happiness of an individual."

*

"By seeing London, I have seen as much of life as the world can show."

*

"I had rather see the portrait of a dog that I know, than all the allegorical paintings they can show me in the world."

*

"Of all noises, I think music is the least disagreeable."

*

"I would be loath to speak ill of any person who I do not know deserves it, but I am afraid he is an attorney."

*

"A am a great friend of public amusements, they keep people from vice."

*

"The return of my birthday, if I remember it, fills me with thoughts which it seems to be the general care of humanity to escape."

*

"I look upon every day to be lost, in which I do not make a new acquaintance."

ABOUT MANKIND

"If a man does not make new acquaintances as he advances through life, he will soon find himself left alone. A man, sir, should keep his friendship in a constant repair."

*

"There are some sluggish men who are improved by drinking; as there are fruits that are not good until they are rotten."

*

"The world is seldom what it seems; to man, who

dimly sees, realities appear as dreams, and dreams realities."

*

"There is nothing, Sir, too little for so little a creature as man. It is by studying little things that we attain the great art of having as little misery and as much happiness as possible."

*

"He who has so little knowledge of human nature as to seek happiness by changing anything but his own disposition will waste his life in fruitless efforts."

*

"A man of genius has been seldom ruined but by himself."

*

"Were it not for imagination a man would be as happy in arms of a chambermaid as of a duchess."

*

"Almost all absurdity of conduct arises from the imitation of those who we cannot resemble."

*

"Patriotism is the last refuge of the scoundrel."

*

"He who waits to do a great deal of good at once will never do anything."

*

"Wine makes a man more pleased with himself; I do not say it makes him more pleasing to others."

*

"Every man has a right to utter what he thinks truth,

and every other man has a right to knock him down for it. Martyrdom is the test."

*

"We love to expect, and when expectation is either disappointed or gratified, we want to be again expecting."

*

"All travel has its advantages. If the passenger visits better countries, he may learn to improve his own. And if fortune carries him to worse, he may learn to enjoy it."

*

"Curiosity is one of the most permanent and certain characteristics of a vigorous intellect."

*

"Nothing flatters a man as much as the happiness of his wife; he is always proud of himself as the source of it."

*

"Few enterprises of great labour or hazard would be undertaken if we had not the power of magnifying the advantages we expect from them."

*

"To strive with difficulties, and to conquer them, is the highest human felicity."

*

"We are long before we are convinced that happiness is never to be found, and each believes it possessed by others, to keep alive the hope of obtaining it for himself."

*

"The chains of habit are too weak to be felt until they are too strong to be broken."

*

"Bachelors have consciences, married men have wives."

*

"You teach your daughters the diameters of the planets and wonder when you are done that they do not delight in your company."

*

"The true measure of a man is how he treats someone who can do him absolutely no good."

*

"No man will be a sailor who has contrivance enough to get himself into a jail; for being in a ship is being in a jail, with the chance of being drowned... a man in a jail has more room, better food, and commonly better company."

*

"Every man is rich or poor according to the proportion between his desires and his enjoyments."

*

"There are minds so impatient of inferiority that their gratitude is a species of revenge, and they return benefits, not because recompense is a pleasure, but because obligation is a pain."

*

"It is not true that people are naturally equal for no two people can be together for even a half an hour without one acquiring an evident superiority over the other."

*

"A fly, Sir, may sting a stately horse and make him wince; but, one is but an insect, and the other is a horse still."

*

"When a man knows he is to be hanged in a fortnight, it concentrates his mind wonderfully."

*

"Integrity without knowledge is weak and useless, and knowledge without integrity is dangerous and dreadful."

*

"He that fails in his endeavors after wealth or power will not long retain either honesty or courage."

*

"The advice that is wanted is commonly not welcome and that which is not wanted, evidently an effrontery."

*

"Almost every man wastes part of his life attempting to display qualities which he does not possess."

*

"Nature has given women so much power that the law has very wisely given them little."

*

"There are few things that we so unwillingly give up, even in advanced age, as the supposition that we still have the power of ingratiating ourselves with the fair sex."

*

"There is nothing which has yet been contrived by man, by which so much happiness is produced as by a good tavern."

*

"A man who has not been in Italy is always

conscious of an inferiority."

*

"When men come to like a sea-life, they are not fit to live on land."

*

"Subordination tends greatly to human happiness. Were we all upon an equality, we should have no other enjoyment than mere animal pleasure."

*

"Wine gives a man nothing... it only puts in motion what had been locked up in frost."

*

"He who praises everybody, praises nobody."

*

"A man is in general better pleased when he has a good dinner upon his table, than when his wife talks Greek."

*

"A wise man is cured of ambition by ambition itself; his aim is so exalted that riches, office, fortune and favour cannot satisfy him."

*

"When a man says he had pleasure with a woman he does not mean conversation."

*

"No man was ever great by imitation."

*

"He who does not mind his belly, will hardly mind anything else."

*

"By taking a second wife he pays the highest
compliment to the first, by showing that she made
him so happy as a married man, that he wishes to be
so a second time."

*

"To get a name can happen but to few; it is one of
the few things that cannot be brought. It is the free
gift of mankind, which must be deserved before it
will be granted, and is at last unwillingly
bestowed."

*

"Depend upon it that if a man talks of his
misfortunes there is something in them that is not
disagreeable to him; for where there is nothing but
pure misery there never is any recourse to the
mention of it."

*

"A man seldom thinks with more earnestness of anything than he does of his dinner."

*

"He that undervalues himself will undervalue others, and he that undervalues others will oppress them."

*

"At seventy-seven it is time to be in earnest."

*

"I have always considered it as treason against the great republic of human nature, to make any man's virtues the means of deceiving him."

*

"A man may be so much of everything that he is nothing of anything."

*

"The wretched have no compassion, they can do good only from strong principles of duty."

*

"Adversity has ever been considered the state in which a man most easily becomes acquainted with himself."

*

"We are inclined to believe those whom we do not know because they have never deceived us."

ABOUT MONEY

"Resolve not to be poor: whatever you have, spend less. Poverty is a great enemy to human happiness; it certainly destroys liberty, and it makes some virtues impracticable, and others extremely difficult."

*

"What makes all doctrines plain and clear? About two hundred pounds a year. And that which was proved true before, prove false again? Two hundred more."

*

"All the arguments which are brought to represent poverty as no evil show it evidently to be a great evil."

*

"Small debts are like small shot; they are rattling on every side, and can scarcely be escaped without a wound: great debts are like cannon; of loud noise, but little danger."

*

"There are few ways in which a man can be more innocently employed than in getting money."

*

"Let me smile with the wise, and feed with the rich."

*

"Without frugality none can be rich, and with it

very few would be poor."

*

"Money and time are the heaviest burdens of life, and... the unhappiest of all mortals are those who have more of either than they know how to use."

*

"To be idle and to be poor have always been reproaches, and therefore every man endeavors with his utmost care to hide his poverty from others, and his idleness from himself."

*

"No money is better spent than what is laid out for domestic satisfaction."

*

"You cannot spend money in luxury without doing good to the poor. Nay, you do more good to them by spending it in luxury, than by giving it; for by

spending it in luxury, you make them exert industry,
whereas by giving it, you keep them idle."

*

"Getting money is not all a man's business: to
cultivate kindness is a valuable part of the business
of life."

*

"It is better to live rich than to die rich."

*

"Agriculture not only gives riches to a nation, but
the only riches she can call her own."

GENERAL PHILOSOPHY

"Nothing is more hopeless than a scheme of
merriment."

*

"Nothing will ever be attempted if all possible
objections must first be overcome."

*

"Promise, large promise, is the soul of an
advertisement."

*

"What is easy is seldom excellent."

*

"There are charms made only for distant admiration."

*

"Bounty always receives part of its value from the manner in which it is bestowed."

*

"Friendship, like love, is destroyed by long absence, though it may be increased by short intermissions."

*

"Courage is the greatest of all virtues, because if you haven't courage, you may not have an opportunity to use any of the others."

*

"When any calamity has been suffered the first thing to be remembered is, how much has been escaped."

*

"The true art of memory is the art of attention."

*

"You can't be in politics unless you can walk in a room and know in a minute who's for you and who's against you."

*

"Everything that enlarges the sphere of human powers, that shows man he can do what he thought he could not do, is valuable."

*

"It is more from carelessness about truth than from intentionally lying that there is so much falsehood in the world."

*

"It is dangerous for mortal beauty, or terrestrial virtue, to be examined by too strong a light. The torch of Truth shows much that we cannot, and all that we would not, see."

*

"Of the blessings set before you make your choice, and be content."

*

"To love one that is great, is almost to be great one's self."

*

"No man can taste the fruits of autumn while he is delighting his scent with the flowers of spring."

*

"Where grief is fresh, any attempt to divert it only irritates."

*

"It generally happens that assurance keeps an even pace with ability."

*

"It is reasonable to have perfection in our eye that we may always advance toward it, though we know it can never be reached."

*

"Praise, like gold and diamonds, owes its value only to its scarcity."

*

"It is better to suffer wrong than to do it, and happier to be sometimes cheated than not to trust."

*

"The feeling of friendship is like that of being comfortably filled with roast beef; love, like being enlivened with champagne."

*

"It is better that some should be unhappy rather than that none should be happy, which would be the case in a general state of equality."

*

"The vanity of being known to be trusted with a secret is generally one of the chief motives to disclose it."

*

"Many things difficult to design prove easy to performance."

*

"If pleasure was not followed by pain, who would forbear it?"

*

"So many objections may be made to everything, that nothing can overcome them but the necessity of doing something."

*

"Love is the wisdom of the fool and the folly of the wise."

*

"To be happy at home is the ultimate result of all ambition, the end to which every enterprise and labour tends, and of which every desire prompts the prosecution."

*

"Revenge is an act of passion; vengeance of justice. Injuries are revenged; crimes are avenged."

*

"Worth seeing? Yes; but not worth going to see."

*

"The two offices of memory are collection and distribution."

*

"Allow children to be happy in their own way, for what better way will they find?"

*

"To keep your secret is wisdom; but to expect others to keep it is folly."

*

"Kindness is in our power, even when fondness is not."

*

"Adversity leads us to think properly of our state, and so is most beneficial to us."

*

"What we hope ever to do with ease, we must learn first to do with diligence."

*

"Between falsehood and useless truth there is little difference. As gold which he cannot spend will make no man rich, so knowledge which cannot apply will make no man wise."

*

"My dear friend, clear your mind of can't."

*

"If your determination is fixed, I do not counsel you to despair. Few things are impossible to diligence and skill. Great works are performed not by strength, but perseverance."

*

"He that will enjoy the brightness of sunshine, must quit the coolness of the shade."

*

"Whoever thinks of going to bed before twelve o'clock is a scoundrel."

*

"Melancholy, indeed, should be diverted by every means but drinking."

*

"Self-confidence is the first requisite to great undertakings."

*

"Exercise is labor without weariness."

*

"There are goods so opposed that we cannot seize both, but, by too much prudence, may pass between them at too great a distance to reach either."

*

"Leisure and curiosity might soon make great advances in useful knowledge, were they not diverted by minute emulation and laborious trifles."

*

"Actions are visible, though motives are secret."

*

"The usual fortune of complaint is to excite contempt more than pity."

*

"Power is not sufficient evidence of truth."

*

"There is, indeed, nothing that so much seduces reason from vigilance, as the thought of passing life with an amiable woman."

*

"Treating your adversary with respect is striking soft in battle."

*

"Love is only one of many passions."

*

"The use of travelling is to regulate imagination by reality, and instead of thinking how things may be, to see them as they are."

*

"All theory is against freedom of the will; all experience for it."

ON LIFE & DEATH

"From the middle of life onward, only he remains
vitally alive who is ready to die with life."

*

"Disease generally begins that equality which death
completes."

*

"A wise man will make haste to forgive, because he
knows the true value of time, and will not suffer it
to pass away in unnecessary pain."

*

"The future is purchased by the present."

*

"Life affords no higher pleasure than that of surmounting difficulties, passing from one step of success to another, forming new wishes and seeing them gratified."

*

"It matters not how a man dies, but how he lives. The act of dying is not of importance, it lasts so short a time."

*

"The mind is never satisfied with the objects immediately before it, but is always breaking away from the present moment, and losing itself in schemes of future felicity... The natural flights of the human mind are not from pleasure to pleasure, but from hope to hope."

*

"Those who attain any excellence, commonly spend
life in one pursuit; for excellence is not often gained
upon easier terms."

*

"Prepare for death, if here at night you roam, and
sign your will before you sup from home."

*

"Life is not long, and too much of it must not pass
in idle deliberation how it shall be spent."

*

"Some desire is necessary to keep life in motion,
and he whose real wants are supplied must admit
those of fancy."

*

"When making your choice in life, do not neglect to live."

*

"Human life is everywhere a state in which much is to be endured, and little to be enjoyed."

*

"Surely a long life must be somewhat tedious, since we are forced to call in so many trifling things to help rid us of our time, which will never return."

*

"The world is like a grand staircase, some are going up and some are going down."

*

"Such is the state of life, that none are happy but by the anticipation of change: the change itself is nothing; when we have made it, the next wish is to change again."

*

"Life is a progress from want to want, not from enjoyment to enjoyment."

*

"Life cannot subsist in society but by reciprocal concessions."

*

"It is a most mortifying reflection for a man to consider what he has done, compared to what he might have done."

*

"You find no man, at all intellectual, who is willing to leave London. No, Sir, when a man is tired of London, he is tired of life; for there is in London all that life can afford."

*

"The happiest part of a man's life is what he passes
lying awake in bed in the morning."

*

"Man alone is born crying, lives complaining, and
dies disappointed."

*

"The love of life is necessary to the vigorous
prosecution of any undertaking."

WORDS & LITERATURE

"No man but a blockhead ever wrote except for money."

*

"The chief glory of every people arises from its authors."

*

"Read over your compositions, and when you meet a passage which you think is particularly fine, strike it out."

45

*

"What is written without effort is in general read without pleasure."

*

"Books like friends should be few and well-chosen."

*

"In order that all men may be taught to speak the truth, it is necessary that all likewise should learn to hear it."

*

"Your manuscript is both good and original; but the part that is good is not original, and the part that is original is not good."

*

"The greatest part of a writer's time is spent in reading in order to write. A man will turn over half a library to make a book."

*

"Words are but the signs of ideas."

*

"Poetry is the art of uniting pleasure with truth."

*

"A man ought to read just as inclination leads him, for what he reads as a task will do him little good."

*

"Language is the dress of thought."

*

"Knowledge is of two kinds. We know a subject ourselves, or we know where we can find information upon it."

*

"One of the disadvantages of wine is that it makes a man mistake words for thoughts."

*

"Dictionaries are like watches, the worst is better than none and the best cannot be expected to go quite true."

*

"The happiest conversation is that of which nothing is distinctly remembered, but a general effect of pleasing impression."

*

"Paradise Lost is a book that, once put down, is

very hard to pick up again."

*

"Classical quotation is the parole of literary men all
over the world."

*

"No place affords a more striking conviction of the
vanity of human hopes than a public library."

*

"Nobody can write the life of a man but those who
have eat and drunk and lived in social intercourse
with him."

*

"You hesitate to stab me with a word, and know not
- silence is the sharper sword."

*

"A man will turn over half a library to make one book."

*

"Books that you carry to the fire, and hold readily in your hand, are most useful after all."

ALSO BY ALICIA BRENT

A Little Book Of Christmas

Dead Interesting

Ellen White Speaks Out

Sugar-Free Smoothies For The Fast Diet

Resolutions And Reflections For The New Year

www.ingramcontent.com/pod-product-compliance
Lightning Source LLC
Chambersburg PA
CBHW070624290526
45790CB00002B/977